RECONSIDER LOVE

LLOYD J. AVERILL

DRAWINGS BY
DAPHNE K. MORRIS

PAN PRESS

LIBRARY OF CONGRESS CATALOG CARD NUMBER
95-071169

ISBN 1-881908-13-5

Order from:

SOUNDVIEW BOOKS
POST OFFICE BOX 60214
SEATTLE, WASHINGTON 98160

Published by:

PAN PRESS
3430 PACIFIC AVE. SE
SUITE A-6, BOX #154
WASHINGTON 98501

In memory of Jeanne, first love,

and for the others I have loved—

Deo gratia!

For Jenni-Lynn
and Robert

with admiration
and respect.

Lloyd

1 November 1996

About the Author

Among Lloyd J. Averill's nine other books are works on higher education, sociology, theology, and Northwest Coast Native art.

Since 1951 he has taught religious studies at both undergraduate and graduate levels, and is now senior lecturer emeritus in the University of Washington.

Acknowledgements

Sections in the chapter on "Love and Marriage" were originally prepared as homilies for the weddings of Diane Bunting and Loren White, Patricia Cosgrove and Greg Watson, Leila Ramac and John Pasco, Shelley Pasco and Jun Akutsu, Betty Austin and David Stephens, Ginevra Cohn and David Strang, Carrie Thompson and Jim Leath, Paula McArdle and Chris Vondrasek, Barbara Iliff and Mark Brotherton, and Mary Truckey and Dan Shaw; for the wedding commemoration of Carla Holm and David Martens; and for the twenty-fifth wedding anniversary of Katie and Duane Pasco. In reproducing the reflections here, I express my gratitude to those good friends for the privilege of participating in the celebration of their coming together.

I want to express gratitude to some very special people: to Carol White, who has taught me more about loving relationships than she will ever know; and to Ruth and Larry Barrett, Maureen and Spencer Bennett, Gail and Ed Crouch, Julie Davis, James DeLong, Gary Dorrien, Leslie Graham, Marion and Conrad

Hilberry, Carrol Hoskins, Robyn Hunt and Steven Pearson, Jan Jacobson, Lisa Jankanish, Debra Jarvis, Bill Kelly, Fran and John Lewis, Paula McArdle, Susan MacDonald, Mary McMahon-Schwartz, Elizabeth Mitchell, Daphne Morris, Jane and Frank Kelsey, Rusty Palmer, Katie Pasco, Hazel Philp, Irene Piekarski, Martha Price, Miriam Smith, and Leona Stuckey-Abbott, who have helped me to make this book clearer and truer. And I want to acknowledge my appreciation for the warm encouragement of publication provided by Marcus Borg, and by Mary and Reah Dougherty, David Shull, Peter Ilgenfritz, and other friends at Seattle's University Congregational United Church of Christ.

My gratitude also goes to Paula McArdle for her assistance with the book's graphic design, and to Daphne Morris for her sensitive and skillful illustrations on the cover and on the title page of each chapter that follows. In those drawings of a Morning Glory, from rootlet through stages of growth to full flowering and seed pod, she has provided a graceful visual metaphor for love.

Some of the material in what follows has been adapted from the chapter on "Crisis in Sexuality: The Loss of the Other" in my book, *The Problem of Being Human* (Judson Press).

Sources of material quoted in the chapters that follow are cited in the concluding section entitled "Notes on Writers and Books."

Introduction

This book is for anyone who is in love, at whatever age or stage.

Unlike many books currently on the market, intended to help people do something about dysfunctional relationships, this one is for the vast majority of lovers who are not in neurotic, addictive, or dangerous situations.

For this larger group of normal lovers, the risk is primarily that of being discouraged too soon by their inexperience, by their quite understandable hesitations, uncertainties, and occasional failures; of giving up prematurely because they have been beguiled by the popular notion that love is just "doing what comes naturally," or by contemporary expectations of instant gratification or instant orgasmic transformation.

What these normal lovers need is not a course in self-therapy but thoughtful, realistic, direct, and engaging insight into what a normal loving relationship takes, and what it gives. So it is addressed to those who are trying to understand and deepen their own personal loves.

No abstract treatise, its series of brief chapters come out of my own personal, and sometimes painful, experiences with love.

The only good reason for an author to write candidly out of his own experience is the expectation that readers may find themselves in his account; will discover, in the mirror images of themselves there, a perspective which can bring them to new awareness.

In the present case, it is not that my experience of love has been exemplary, or that my reflections on it possess any special authority. Rather, in identifying with my experience, readers may find companionship in their perplexities about love and, provoked by what I have written, may find fresh imagination and courage for shaping their own loving strategies.

The chapters that follow are intentionally brief. My hope is that each will serve as a provocation, for thoughtful consideration by an individual reader, or even better for shared reading and reflection by lovers.

The poems included here were originally written under the immediate influence of some intense experience, and at the time they had the effect both of compacting and sharpening that experience, and of freeing me for more understanding and loving response to it. I recommend that kind of writing. Most of them were originally written, at most, for an intended audience of one; some were written for my own reflection only. They are included in this book because they add greater personal directness and existential intensity to the prose discourse that surrounds them, and because they may encourage lovers to risk their own poetic venturing.

Nearly thirty years ago, a young woman named Carolyn King, one of my students at Kalamazoo College, wrote a line that impressed me then as expressing in remarkably compact form an essential truth about our human condition. It has stayed with me all this time, and it provides a kind of text for everything that follows:

"Who is not ready ever for love, is not."

—Lloyd J. Averill
Seattle, Washington

Contents

ONE

Locating Love

Love's Faces

$\mathcal{W}$hat is the "love" which readers of this small volume are invited to "reconsider"? In spite of its complexity and mystery, in these days particularly we need to try to say what we mean by it, because we are living in a time when the word itself has become trivialized, virtually emptied of reliable meaning.

This is a book written for lovers, for those who have been possessed—who have been filled and fulfilled—by that strange and wonderful attraction which makes it possible for two people at least to consider an exclusive and unqualified commitment to each other. Putting it that way may sound a bit old-fashioned. Of course, even the most solid of relationships are touched by anxieties and uncertainties. Yet in the end, anything less than a willingness to enter into an exclusive commitment to each other is more likely to be evidence of self-indulgence or exploitation rather than of love; and any relationship that is less than whole-hearted, quite literally, is in trouble from the start.

In view of the rather indiscriminate, sometimes confusing variety of applications of the word love in our contemporary usage, it may be useful and refreshing to look again at the four quite different words the ancient Greeks used to designate the distinctive "faces" of love. What the readers of this book are invited to reconsider is a love which encompasses—integrates, embodies—all four.

There was *eros*, which did not necessarily mean sexual love, as more modern usage would lead us to assume, but rather more broadly, *the love of the lovely.* It was the love of that which was so powerfully attractive, so desirable, that one wanted to possess it and to be possessed by it, not physically but spiritually or aesthetically.

There was *philia,* which meant *friendship,* the love of those who are bonded by shared outlooks, interests, origins, commitments.

There was *epithymia,* explicitly *sexual self-giving,* mutual sensual pleasuring.

And there was, finally *agape,* the distinctive word for love in the New Testament, which means *"love in spite of"*—respect and caring for the full humanity of the other, even when, in times of unattractiveness and disappointment, even of conflict, there seems to be little to like. In the New Testament it is love even for the enemy.

The only kind of love that is likely to sustain and enrich two people in their totality, the only kind of love that has staying power, the only kind of love that has the slightest chance of becoming and remaining exclusive and unqualified, is one that includes all four of these. Relationships regularly get into trouble when one or another of them is absent, or when one or two come to predominate, to crowd out the others. *Eros*—attractiveness, genuine liking of each other—is the foundation. *Philia*—common bonds—shifts the focus importantly from each other to a shared world. *Epithymia*—sexual intimacy—gives the relationship its emotional intensity and depth. And *agape*—care for each other that is deeper than liking and bonding, cooler and more deliberate than sexual excitement—sustains us in those moments of disappointment and conflict which mark even the best of relationships.

Only love in this larger sense is worth reconsidering.

And that, on the face of it, looks pretty nearly impossible. Who can even find all of those strands in her, in his, own experience; and even if found, who is sensitive enough, selfless enough, steadfast enough to gather them into a livable unity? None of us, taken by ourselves. But the remarkable thing—the miracle, if you will—is that it does happen, more often than popular impressions of widespread relational dysfunction would lead us to think. If not always and everywhere, it happens here and there, now and then.

This book is, if not a guide, at least a witness to the possibility of that miracle.

Love: "In," or on its way "out"?

Love, these days, is "in."

Evidence for its "in-ness" is found on the most sacred icons of our culture: T-shirts, bumper stickers, postage stamps, and billboards that tell us "Love is a loan from Fidelity Savings Bank."

It is sometimes announced in the most unexpected of ways. A male undergraduate of my acquaintance picked a name at random from the local telephone directory, dialled the number, and said without preliminary to the startled subscriber on the other end of the line, "I love you!"

It happened, by the happiest of accidents, that the subscriber was a lonely widow 72 years of age, who was touched by this unexpected avowal because no one had said "I love you!" to her in 10 years. If, instead, the one receiving the call had been a middle-aged male who suspected his wife of having an affair, there might have been a very unhappy accident—had the husband been able to find out who the caller was.

On a promotional spot for a local public television station, physician and author Bernie Siegel reported that a member of the Arizona State Senate stopped business in that chamber in order to be able to say, "I love you," individually to each member of that body, transforming 22 hardened and cynical politicians into a roomful of warm fuzzies, if Dr. Siegel is to be believed.

In spite of the varied signs that love is "in"—or perhaps because of the saturation of those signs; even more particularly because of the indiscriminate, careless, often quite trivial way the word itself is used—I'm apprehensive that our popular preoccupation with love may be so far "in" that it is, in fact, on its way "out." "In-ness" often has just that consequence. As a Kingsley Amis character says in *The Russian Girl*, "if all sorts of things were going to be deemed to be love, then there would be less of the actual thing to go around."

Sic transit gloria mundi,* someone may be tempted to reply. After a time, even the most sublime experience begins to bore. Why should we expect it to be otherwise in our current love affair with love?

Why indeed? Yet surely there is something that we ought more than ordinarily to regret if this current preoccupation should turn out to be merely another fad that goes as quickly and unregrettably as it came. Some years ago the poet Archibald MacLeish warned that we are living in a time of "the diminishment of the human." If only each of us knew, now, how to keep love alive and growing—even if only with one other person—this could become the generation known in history for its refusal to yield to our human diminishment, and for our insistence on seeing our human kind restored to the image in and for which we are made.

For we are made by Love for love: that spiritual affirmation joins many religious traditions, and it conveys the most profound truth about ourselves. A person unloving and unloved is a person diminished, undistinguished from the meanest object in creation. A person loving and loved is a person completed, the crown of the creative possibilities our Creator has placed within our reach. Oddly enough, the real nemesis of love at this particular moment of human history is probably not anything so dramatic as the orga-

---

*   *"So passes away the glory of the world."*

nized power of some new cynicism, or of some rampant new hate. Simple disillusionment may be enough to bring to an end the current openness toward love. I'm afraid that many who have been attracted by love's bright promise may have embraced it without really understanding it, and may be ready to give it up prematurely: may think that it does not work because they have not worked at it; may think themselves ready for love's conjugal nakedness when it is moral nakedness love requires; may not understand that love not only gives but expects; may refuse to risk the pain love may entail.

These are some of the things this small book is about. If, rather than consent to a fading fad, we are to keep love alive and growing—in our own intimate relationships, and in the broader human community as well—we shall have to reconsider love.

TWO

Love's Pitfalls
& Perils

Love In A Lonely Time

There is a peculiar bias in our times that makes it especially difficult to reconsider love; a bias that makes it more essential than ever to get on at once with that reconsideration.

Now and then in history a generation comes along to insist that the basic human unit is one person; that tries to live wholly within the self, as if no one else mattered; that has to learn from its own sad mistakes that aloneness does not result in wholeness; instead that aloneness results, at best, in half a life.

This is such a time. There are those, just now, who believe that it's possible to be a complete self quite independently of any other self or selves—in other words, that selfhood is, in significant measure, a lonely achievement.

A decade ago a research study, tellingly entitled *Habits of the Heart*, called such people "expressive individualists." At a time when millions of Americans have sought help in psychotherapy, this study concluded that the kind of relationship that exists between a therapist and a client has become the accepted model for all intimate relationships—among friends, between parent and child, between lovers.

And what does that therapeutic model look like? With a few notable and important exceptions, said *Habits of the Heart*, the typical relationship between client and therapist lacks symmetry, lacks real mutuality. In the therapeutic situation there is a unique combination of intimacy and distance, but only one party—the client—is intimate; the therapist rarely discloses anything of herself as a person.

One party—the client—talks, while the other—the therapist—listens. It's an instrumental relationship, focussed exclusively on what happens in and to the client, rather than having an outcome in which both therapist and client have a lasting stake. And it tries to bring about psychic healing by detaching the client from his relationships in the isolation of the therapist's office.

In the therapeutic situation, as it is widely practiced, there's no morality which is not of the client's own choosing: no external "shoulds" or "oughts," no independent right or wrong, good or evil, which has any claim on the client's life, as the client is repeatedly reminded.

So the client constitutes his own moral universe. Therapy tries to help him clarify exactly what he feels, exactly what he wants. And his only obligation to others is to tell them, as clearly as he can, just what it is that he feels and wants.

The researchers who wrote *Habits of the Heart* concluded that it is a "cultural fiction" to believe that "we not only can, but must, make up our deepest beliefs in the isolation of our private selves." Yet this fiction—based on a therapeutic model that is asymmetrical, detached, self-centered, unresponsive, and irresponsible—sets the terms on which many Americans, in and out of therapy, understand themselves and try to order their relationships.

Should we be surprised that therapy on these terms regularly falls short of permanent resolution; that it often goes on and on; that clients move through their lives from one therapist to another in an endless quest for fulfillment?

Should we be surprised that so-called relationships influenced by that model—between lovers, between parent and child, among friends—are shallow, fragile, unsatisfying, impermanent? In lives shaped by that model there are no permanent bonds or shared meanings; and without shared meanings, there can be no permanent bonds, so life becomes a series of momentary encounters at best, or falls into a desperate loneliness at worst.

Cain, the slayer of Abel, was history's first "expressive individualist," the prototype of all those who, ever since, have failed to understand that their own destiny is entailed in the destiny of the other; that selfhood is not a closing in but a reaching out. When God asked the whereabouts of the missing Abel after Cain had killed him, Cain replied with callous evasiveness, "Am I my brother's keeper?"

It would have been enough if he had merely been his brother's brother.

Love Is Hard Work

The confusion of loneliness with integrity that marks our times is by no means love's only peril. Popular romantic, oversimplified, sadly mistaken notions of love create false expectations that lead to disillusionment and often to disaster.

One such notion is that love is effortless; that it is a natural talent, a spontaneous welling up and reaching out, over which no conscious control can be exercised. Relationships regularly come apart around that fallacy. When one marriage partner discovers that his feeling for his mate has changed, he often accepts that change passively, as if it ought to be so if it is so. And if asked about it, he may simply reply, "My feelings are different now. I just don't love her any more," as if that statement had a kind of self-evident conclusiveness, a kind of moral adequacy, about which there is nothing more to be said or done.

But it's a mistake to believe, as we so commonly do, that behavior must follow after feelings, that we can't act unless we have first felt; that I can't—indeed, that I needn't—act lovingly if I don't first feel loving.

The fact is that our feelings often follow where our behavior has first led. Anyone knows that who has ever taken up a point of view in an informal argument, or in a formal debate, not because she has any real feeling for the view but just for the sake of the argument. Entering enthusiastically into the game, she tries skillfully to turn aside the objections of her opponent and to fashion persuasive support for her adopted view.

And often the result is that what began as an exercise ends up as a conviction: the reasoning and the evidence she has managed to turn up in the course of the debate may have something to do with the change of heart, to be sure. But equally important, the player discovers, in the course of imitating the behavior of a person of particular conviction, that she is able to carry off that imitation competently; and more important, that she likes the way that behavior feels.

Thus is imitation transmuted into authenticity.

So love, I'm now sure, is a practiced response to life. Love always requires some degree of self-displacement to make room for the beloved, and self-displacement is never easy. It has to be worked at. To focus deliberately on the full sound of another's voice takes enormous discipline, given as we sometimes are to the prepossessing notion that our own voices are the most compelling sounds in creation.

Because love is a practiced response to life, love means having to say "I love you" and to act out the meaning of those words even at moments when I don't feel very much like it. And to do so is not so much hypocrisy as it is an exercise in self-fulfilling prophecy: it's the imitation that produces the reality.

There was a time when I found it offensive to speak of "making love." That sounded too contrived and mechanical, and I was sure that love could only be love if it were spontaneous and unrehearsed. Now I take a quite different view of the matter. Kingsley Amis was right, I think, in what he did with the lovers in his novel *I Want It Now.* As one reviewer described it, Amis "has Ronnie and Simon imitate love for selfish reasons until pretense becomes the real thing."

Perhaps we would all agree that love is an art. But the trouble with all great art is that it appears deceptively easy. Whenever I hear the choir of Kings College, Cambridge, at Evensong in the magnificent 15th century college chapel, I am stunned by the apparent effortlessness of the sound. The clarity of tone, the liquidity of line, the elevation of mood that soars to the fan-vaulted ceiling and beyond, all seem in that moment to be of celestial origin.

Yet the truth is that such perfection of artistry is the product of untold hours of rehearsal, and of a disciplined sublimation of each chorister to the tempo and temperament of the music. Though it's far from the popular view of the matter, there is in all great art not only the ecstasy of spontaneous creation but the agony of hard work.

And so it is with love: Who does not work at it will not be found by it.

THE COURSE OF TRUE LOVE NE'ER DID RUN SMOOTH

Life has been flat these weeks since you said,
"I've got to pull back for a while."
Tasteless. Gone to sadness and sighing. Empty—
except for haunting images of lost loveliness.
"I'll wait for you to call," I had replied.
Against all longing, I kept that promise.
Five weeks I kept it, against all desire, all impulse,
hoping you would call and end my exile.
Until last night I kept it. But after five weeks,
I had to know. Whatever the risk that you might
speak a word I desperately didn't want to hear,
I had to know—to put an end to agony.

So I called, finger hardly daring to dial,
voice at the edge of trembling, heart racing.
You answered, softly as always. "How are you?"
you asked. No mere convention, that, for the
sound of you—the marvelous inflection of you
that in earlier days had made love to me without
meaning to—conveyed warmth, caring, real wanting
to know.

That one question was more than I dared hope for.
Nor was it all you said:
"I've thought about you. I've missed you.
I want to see you. How about Friday?"
Those words have echoed in my heart, these
intervening hours. Incredible.
Life has been flat these weeks since you said,
"I've got to pull back for a while."
Then last night: surprised by joy!.
Our Friday is only thirty-six hours away,
but this morning it feels like forever.

Good agony this time!

Love Expects

There is a strange but popularly romantic notion that the lover gives freely to the beloved, but never sets expectations for the beloved; that love yields but never awaits.

Not so. The fact is that genuine love always creates expectations for the beloved, and where there are no expectations, there is no love.

The French philosopher Gabriel Marcel is the one who has helped me to see this truth most clearly. Here's what Marcel said:

> My relationship to myself is mediated by the presence of the other person, by what he is for me and I am for him. To love anybody is to expect something from him....[I]t is at the same time in some way to make it possible for him to fulfill his expectation. Yes, paradoxical as it may seem, to expect is in some ways to give; but the opposite is nonetheless true; no longer to expect is to strike with sterility the being from whom no more is expected. It is then in some way to deprive him or take from him in advance what is surely a certain possibility of inventing or of creating. Everything looks as though we can only speak of hope where the interaction exists between him who gives and him who receives.

For me to love, Marcel suggests, is to expect something of my beloved. To be loved is to have something expected of me. When something is expected of me, I am given hope, because the very fact of the confidence expressed in me by that expectation confers on me power to fulfill what is expected. When I love another, the expectation created by my love is a source of hope and power for the other.

I am deprived of hope when the other no longer expects anything of me. No longer to expect anything of the other is to rob that other of hope.

In fact, Marcel makes the point even more strongly: "...no longer to expect is to strike with sterility the being from whom no more is expected." There is nothing more devastating for a child than to discover, by the most subtle or the most egregious of signs, that his parents have given up expecting anything more of him; for an aging parent to discover that his adult child has given up expecting anything more of him; for a woman to discover that her partner has given up expecting anything more of her. When these things happen, verbal declarations of love by parents, by adult child, by partner, cannot hide the fact of an abandonment that is, in its way, more terrifying than overt repudiation would be.

When hope is withdrawn, love is an empty word.

The Abuse of Love

I have a friend, a serious Christian, who believed that, if she were to be faithful to the familiar description in I Corinthians 13— that "love suffers long and is kind"—it would mean tolerating the physical depredations of her abusive husband.

It doesn't!

The love for which we have been created, and to which we are called by almost universal spiritual witness, is not one that invites us to ignore our own good. Rather it asks us to will the good of another with the same passion that we will our own, to participate actively in the good of another with the same eagerness that we participate in our own. And no woman participates in the good of another when she permits that other to engage in an abusiveness that is as damaging and dangerous to his spiritual and emotional well-being as it is to her own.

Openness toward another—a willingness to risk the vulnerability without which nothing worth the name of love is possible— means making ourselves accessible to the human need of the other, not to his exploitative battering. And what the abuser needs is to have his abuse stopped, not tolerated.

To be responsible in love for another entails doing with and for the other what we would have that other do with and for ourselves. And that means refusing to accede to the harm the abuser does to himself through the harm he does to the one he abuses.

Love's Other Abuse

There is, in our relatedness, a danger far more subtle, far more insidious, far more common than physical violence. It is our manipulation of each other that we often disguise as love—disguise it from ourselves as well as from the other.

It's simply a fact, against which we must continually struggle, that what begins as love, what touts itself proudly as love, often turns destructive. Love is readily and regularly confused with the attempted absorption of one life by another, the possession of one life by another. What justify themselves as humility and selflessness readily become the most subtle and dangerous forms of aggression against another human being. What begins as service to another is often transformed by imperceptible degrees into condescension, manipulation, control.

Such are the surface similarities between love and absorption, between service and manipulation, and such is our talent for self-deception, that we easily persuade ourselves that we are engaged in the former while wreaking the spiritual havoc of the latter. Thus does love turn destructive, even demonic.

But real love, whatever else it may be, is nothing less than a willingness to live in intimacy while permitting the other to be fully the other. Paradoxically as it may seem, if we are to find a capacity for loving intimacy, we shall have to maintain a certain loving distance from the beloved.

Kahlil Gibran was close to the mark when, in *The Prophet*, he wrote of marriage:

> ...let there be spaces in your togetherness...
> Love one another, but make not a bond of love;
> Let it rather be a moving sea between the shores of
> your souls...
> Sing and dance together and be joyous, but let each
> of you be alone,
> Even as the strings of a lute are alone, though they
> quiver with the same music.
> Give your hearts, but not into each other's keeping
> For only the hand of Life can contain your hearts.

So there's more to love than being close. Love that recognizes and respects the full otherness of the other: nothing short of that will do. There can be no safety in a relationship, whether for loving or being loved, unless there is otherness as well as intimacy.

But how to overcome our human propensity to get too close is the problem. Simple determination of the will by itself is unpromising, since that is likely to rob the relationship of a vital spontaneity. Intellectual self-persuasion misses the mark, because the source of the problem is not in the mind but in the energies of the ego.

I know of no way to address the problem successfully that doesn't entail finding access to spiritual resources; and if for anyone that should be bad news, it's nevertheless the best I can do.

If there is to be otherness as well as intimacy, my self-giving must be lifted up in an act of transcendent mediation. Paul Tillich told us what is necessary in words that reveal his essential theism; others will find a different language more acceptable, but they will need access to the same reality however described. Here are Tillich's words:

> ...we can never reach the innermost center of another being [by direct search or assault]....But we can reach it in a movement that rises first to God and then returns from [God] to the other self. In this way [the need of the other for her own otherness] is not removed, but taken into the community with that in which the centers of all beings rest. Even love is reborn in solitude. For only in solitude are those who are alone able to reach those from whom they are separated....One hour of solitude may bring us closer to those we love than many hours of communication. We can take them with us to the hills of eternity.

Self-Love, Other Love

*O*ne of the things that can throw love off balance—that can lead to behavior toward the one I love that is either dangerously aggressive or dangerously submissive—is a distorted view of my self.

Any of us may experience a temporary loss of self-regard, when we face disappointments or failures and wonder whether or not we are bright enough, or talented enough, or worthy enough, to deserve the things we aspire to. And then we may want someone to take over our lives, to take care of us, to give us the reassurance we are unable to give to ourselves.

Or alternately, any of us may experience a temporary excess of self-regard, when life seems to move our way, when everything seems to fall into place and we succeed even beyond our expectations. And then we may reach out to draw the other into our apparently successful, presumably wise and beneficent but nevertheless controlling ambit.

None of us ever succeeds in living a life perfectly balanced between self-depreciation and self-appreciation, between recessive and excessive modes, and my own judgment is that life so evenly balanced would be an unutterable bore. There are times when I need the caring of another, when it is right and good to put myself trustingly into the hands of the one I love. And there are times when it is good and right for me to accept in trust the life of that loved one. The lives of most of us alternately healthily between the two.

The problem arises when one or the other of these senses of self—excessive self-doubt, excessive self-confidence—predominates in me, distorting my self-understanding and consequently endangering my relationship with the one I love. Excessive self-confidence gives me a good conscience about the abuse of a relationship—if not by overt physical or emotional means, then by covert manipulation and control—on the overweening conviction that I know what is best not only for myself but for the other, and because what fragile selfhood I can manage is taking its substance from the submissiveness of that other to my will.

On the other hand, excessive self-doubt leads me to a willingness to be abused, controlled, manipulated, even when I know those things are happening, on the conviction that my own instincts are not to be trusted, that the other knows what is best for me, and that however abusive the relationship may be, if I were to lose it I would be devastated, destroyed; that what fragile selfhood I have will be nullified and I will be left with no substance at all.

These are desperate and dangerous alternatives. This book, addressed as it is to those who are not in dysfunctional relationships, is not designed to do more than name the condition, and to urge that there can be no real, proportioned love of the other—none that is worthy of the name—unless there is also proportioned love for the self. Psychiatrist James F. Masterson has defined intimacy as:

> the capacity of two people to offer each other's *real* selves affection and acknowledgement in a close, ongoing interpersonal relationship.

Consequently the emerging of the *real* self is of vital im-

portance to the capacity to love another person successfully in a sustained, mutually satisfying relationship. [Em-
phasis added].

The problem with the two personality types sketched above is
that they are seriously defective in that properly-proportioned view
of the self that is the precondition of genuine self-love: the ability
both to accept and affirm one's personal excellences without exaggeration, and to accept and affirm one's personal defects without
exaggeration. And that means, by the reflexive and unvarying law
of human relationships, that those two types are defective in the
ability genuinely to love the other, both accepting and affirming that
other's personal excellences and personal defects without exaggeration.

So when two people find their relationship disappointed, frus-
trated, unbalanced, not just occasionally as any relationship may be,
but regularly, they do well to find competent help in assessing
whether or not, in one or the other or perhaps in both, defective
self-love is the barrier to effective other-love. A useful printed re-
source, among many others that are available, is *The Search for the
Real Self: Unmasking the Personality Disorders of Our Age*, by James
F. Masterson, M.D. (Free Press, 1988).

THREE

Love's Promise

We Need Each Other

AUDITING ART HISTORY 310

Usually she arrives before he does,
saves a seat for him next to hers in the
rapidly filling lecture hall,
watches eagerly for him to appear
among the entering flood of undergraduates.

There he is, moving with brisk purpose
through the flow. He looks for her in the
rising tier of seats, finds her, smiles his
warming smile, takes his place beside her.

This is what they come for three times a week.
The lectures are incidental.

*R*omantic love, in which two people feel themselves ineluctably drawn to each other, is no mere epiphenomenon of the human condition. It is, rather, the surfacing of something deep and permanent, something essential in our human makeup.

As the Jewish philosopher Martin Buber said, "All real life is meeting."

We need each other—need each other quite beyond our wanting each other. The romantic attraction to which we are drawn often seems sudden, surprising, unpremeditated. In fact, the search for the other went on before we knew it; went on quite without our knowing it.

THE SUDDEN FLOWERING OF AN UNEXPECTED SPRING

"Like a teenager in the back seat of a car,"
you said you felt as we kissed last night.

I felt it too—the freshness, the rush, the daring.
Rare feelings for those as experienced as we.
Scarcely believable feelings for two
whose disappointments are still fresh, still edged;
who have wondered if we would—could—
ever feel that way again.

Yet there we were, young lovers rising to passion
as if for the first time,
celebrating our own spring ten days early.

Was it only the romantic impulse of a warming moment?
Fragile infatuation with feelings we have not lately known?
Passing intrigue with the newness of each other?

Deliciously romantic it was.
Intrigue and infatuation happily were there,
deepening arousal. But impulsive, fragile, passing?

We are not as new as we seem, we two.
I have known you for a very long time.
Over months—years even—your image has been growing
clearer in my heart.
How unremarkable, then, that I should have recognized you when
you came, red-coated, to our first meeting
that January Sunday evening a scant two months ago

You are the one I've dreamed of, ached for.
Last night I felt again the astonishing gift of you—
the loveliness, the tenderness,
the reaching out and the taking in
that, all these years, I knew would be there.

When I said, "I love you,"
it was something I have waited to say,
not two months, but a lifetime.

Each of us—as woman, as man—is on a search to discover that which is unknown and strange to us. We have sought our opposite, one who can embody for us what we cannot fully be for ourselves. Each of us has an uncompleted other within the self. In our coming together is the possibility of greater completeness for each of us, of breaking the limitations of being woman, of being man, without being less of either, and thus of becoming more fully human.

So when we truly love, we love not merely with the self, but with the gift the lover gives us.

It is a strange and wonderful thing, that gift we give each other. Should any aspiring lover fear that giving of herself, of himself, will mean a diminution of selfhood, Frederick Buechner tells us how it really is:

By all the laws both of logic and simple arithmetic, to give yourself away in love to another would seem to mean that you end up with less of yourself left than you had to begin with. But the miracle is that just the reverse is true, logic and arithmetic go hang. To give yourself away in love to somebody else...is to become for the first time yourself fully. To live not just for yourself alone anymore but for another self to whom you swear to be true—plight your troth, your truth to—is in a new way to come fully alive. Things needn't have been that way as far as we know, but that is the way things are, that is the way life is, and if you and I are inclined to have any doubts about it, we can always put it to the test. The test, needless to say, is our lives themselves.

Romance Becoming Love

SATURDAY, 4 A.M.

All day I have felt the pace
of my life quicken, as if toward
some fresh promise.

Anticipation, newly edged
since we met a week ago.

Quiet excitement, touching these
last few days with strange and
wonderful resonance.

Sighing, not this time from present
sadness but from the loveliness that
has been absent since we last said goodnight
a scant twenty-four hours ago.

Wakefulness now, prising and
parsing it all out.

Oddest, most unfamiliar,
joy seems to be seeping in.
What's going on here?

Love is the most complex, and in the end the most mysterious, of human experiences. No single phenomenon, it is made up of components we can list but can't exhaust (as in the chapter on "Love's Gifts" below). Although animals show affection, as far as we know love is unique to the human species. It is, in fact, what makes us human, literally in the procreative act of love which gives us birth, and ever after in those myriad loving acts out of which each of us makes a life.

On its romantic side, love is discovery, excitement, even giddiness, anticipation, impatience, delicious agony, passion. Romance is quite wonderful. No love affair should be without it.

THE TIME OF HIS LIFE

Showered. Shaved. Dressed. But no point in
leaving the house for at least an hour. He itches
to move the clock's hands ahead—as if that
would really change the time, bring him to her sooner.

Impatience wins. In less than an hour he's in the
car, out of the drive, down Richmond Beach Road
heading for the ferry landing. Damn! Traffic
signals conspire to keep him from her. They've
never been so slow. Must be a malfunction. If
there were no cross traffic, he'd risk a run on red.
But no such luck. He revs the motor, ready to surge
forward the instant red turns to green.

Now, the ferry line—at its most maddening! No
special day or time, yet the length of cars looks

like Labor Day weekend. Once aboard, he gets
an enticing glimpse of her cottage on the far shore
        just beyond Clamshell Cove. And yet,
"how little more and how much it is, how little
less and it's worlds away."

Finally, the entrance to her drive. With all of his
imagined delays, he's still twenty minutes too soon!
He fidgets beside her mailbox at the top of the lane,
waiting for 900 interminable seconds to pass,
having decided she won't mind if he's five minutes early.

At last. Down the drive. Park. Get out. Knock.
She opens. They embrace.

Now let time stand still.

But a romantic is often merely in love with love, more self-love reflected in the other than other-love refracted in the self. More than that, the problem with romance is that, while the high level on which it feeds can be momentarily recaptured, it can't be sustained indefinitely. Discovery slows, excitement and giddiness lose their edge, impatience becomes more patient and agony and passion lose their intensity. And then, the options are either loving or leaving.

I suspect that leaving is the more frequent precipitate of romance. But when romance is actually transmuted into authentic love, that change is marked by an absolutely essential shift in the focus of the relationship. It is more often a silent growing than the result of deliberate effort. The shift of focus is sometimes so subtle that it happens quite without our knowing it. But what a difference knowing it makes!

SEEING IN LOVE

Love, Antoine de St. Exupéry somewhere wrote,
is not two people looking passionately at each other;
love is two people looking passionately together
at the world.

Did we make love, then, that Sunday in March
when spring drew winter into early warmth?
We saw singularly, you and I. Remember
what we looked at?

> *Black alluvial earth down along the Missouri,*
> *where farmers will have truck with carrot and cabbage*
> *come summer.*

> *A small slum of a state park, wasted by winter*
> *and neglect.*

> *That old, red hand-pump above the distillery spring,*
> *where water turns to spirit.*

> *Can any good come out of Atchison? we railed*
> *as we drove into town.*
> *And then—we saw those magnificent Victorian houses.*
> *The one, lived in, had two giant gargoyles*
> *on its ridge-pole. The other,*
> *turned hospitable gallery for Sunday*
> *visitors like us, was full of polished wood, stained glass,*
> *and memories.*

St. Mary College, *with sheltering trees*
along the winding drive,
like Sisters of Mercy in silent procession
to evening prayer.

Are these the arousing sights that turn friends to lovers?
No more likely, I would have said, than that the day,
which began gray and dour, could hold much promise
for an outing. Yet as we drove, that day
turned bright and warm.

We changed, too—changed from friends to lovers. How else
but by the mysterious kindling of common sight?
That night we came back here and, for the first time,
did what lovers have always done, with no need
of a St. Exupéry to tell us how.

Love & Selfhood

*E*arlier I described the sad bias of our times: the widespread fiction that the basic human unit is one person, that selfhood is a lonely achievement.

The contrasting view—the humanly more expansive view—is that there is no human selfhood except in interdependence with another self or selves—in other words, that selfhood is, in significant measure, a gift.

The Jewish philosopher Martin Buber summarized both Jewish and Christian traditions when he declared, "In the beginning is relation."

Hendrik Ibsen made our need of each other the compelling theme of his drama Peer Gynt. Young Peer was a brawler, a liar, a drunkard, known for his flagrant disregard of almost everyone and everything. Even his mother called him "a hopeless ne'er-do-well" and went to her grave grieving for his wasted life. Solveig, the only other person for whom Peer seemed to have any regard, was repeatedly hurt by his excesses.

There's something too extreme about Peer: his antics are too bizarre, too calculated to shock, his apparent gaiety and wit too desperate. These aren't the acts of one who simply has an excess of youthful exuberance; they are, rather, the actions of a deeply troubled spirit seeking to disguise its trouble.

Early in the drama it becomes clear that Peer is engaged in a frantic and fruitless search for self-significance. In spite of the appearance that he commands life, he admits inwardly that life for him is "empty, ugly, dreary," a dreadful burden. It's a burden he seems unable to share, perhaps because he has a talent for building walls rather than bridges, perhaps because he assumes—as many Americans now assume—that self-significance, if it is achieved at all, must be sought as a lonely prize. So, standing in the night outside a hut in which Solveig waits for him, Peer calls out his desperation with a double meaning Solveig does not quite grasp:

> Solveig: What do you say?
> Peer: Dear, you must wait. It's dark, and I've a heavy load.
> Solveig: I'll come and help you bear the load.
> Peer: No, do not come! Stay where you are! I'll bear the whole of it.
> Solveig: But dear, don't be too long.
> Peer: Be patient, child; whether the time is long or short, you must wait.
> Solveig (nodding to him): Yes, I will wait.

So Peer leaves her to chase his phantom self half-way around the world, through revolution and shipwreck. One day he sits peeling an onion, removing first one layer and then the next, always expecting to find substance at the core; but when the last layer comes away, there is nothing. So it is with his own lonely quest for substance: layer after layer of Peer comes away, but when all are gone, there is only emptiness.

Then after years of wandering it's an aged and sobered Peer Gynt who returns to Solveig. And in the predawn darkness he experiences in their meeting a grace he could not have expected and speaks a confession he would not otherwise have dared:

Solveig: 'Tis he! 'Tis he! Thanks be to God.

Peer: Tell me how sinfully I have offended!…Cry out, cry out my sins aloud.

Solveig (sitting down beside him): You have made my life a beautiful song. Bless you for having come back to me!…

Peer:…I am lost!…Unless you can solve a riddle!

Solveig: What is it?

Peer: What is it? You shall hear. Can you tell me where Peer Gynt has been since last we met?

Solveig: Where he has been?

Peer: With the mark of destiny on his brow—the man that he was when a thought of God's created him? Can you tell me that? If not, I must go to my last home in the land of shadows.

Solveig (smiling): That riddle's easy.

Peer: Tell me, then—where was my real self, complete and true—the Peer that bore the stamp of God upon his brow?

Solveig: In my faith, and in my hope, and in my love.

Peer:…O hide me, hide me in your love!

Nothing I know in life or literature speaks more tellingly than these words to what H. Richard Niebuhr meant when he wrote, "To be able to say that I am I [is to acknowledge] my existence as the counterpart of another self."

Garrison Keillor, in one of his monologues, put it with elegant understatement this way: "It's an amazing thing to be loved by somebody. It's almost just about enough, sometimes. Almost just about enough."

Love As Carnality, 1

The term "carnal" is deliberately chosen here to introduce some reflections on the physical intimacy that is so essentially, so integrally a part of love's fullness; that is so delightfully a source of the joy we awaken in each other in our love.

RAPTURE

Lover, with your lilting voice, your laughing eyes,
Lips that yield and stir, cool hands that bid me wait,
Breasts whose sweetness leaves my tongue intoxicate,
Hidden cleft of love where meet those urging thighs,
Legs that lengthen all the loveliness they lift:
Though a thousand times you've given me your gift,
Lover, never once without some new surprise.

The word "sex" has become so debased these days, that virtually the last thing it connotes is love. So for this discussion it is useful to find another term that is less compromised. At the same time, the alternative must carry a no less primal, fleshly, ecstatic connotation than the word sex did in a more innocent time. Carnal is such a word.

Because carnal connotes "bodily pleasure," it can carry the weight of the intimate connection, and through that connection the intimate communication, two people create in mutual, sensual pleasuring.

It suffers, of course, from assumptions that it has more to do with animal rutting than with spiritual elevation, an assumption I want explicitly to dislodge. There is no ground, in Western religious traditions, for viewing the body and its appetites—and especially its sensual appetites—as inherently debased, as more prone to distortion and misuse than is the mind.

A view that has claimed religious sanction holds that the ideal spiritual person is an asexual being who indulges in coition solely out of reluctant reproductive necessity, if at all. The truth is quite otherwise. There is no incompatibility between the requirements of a godly life and the physical and emotional joys that come to us in our carnality. The body no less than the mind is the vehicle through which we both experience and express spiritual transcendence.

Godliness itself comes to us precisely in and through the carnal. The theologian Dietrich Bonhoeffer emphatically denied the contradiction between carnality and spirituality when he wrote,

> ...speaking frankly, to long for the transcendent when you are in your wife's arms is, to put it mildly, a lack of taste, and it is certainly not what God expects of us. We ought to find God and love him in the blessings he sends us. If he pleases to grant us some overwhelming earthly bliss, we ought not to try and be more religious than God himself. For then we should spoil that bliss by our presumption and arrogance, we should be letting our religious fantasies run riot and refusing to be satisfied with what he gives.

Poetry is a more sensitive, more immediate medium for evoking the realities of ecstasy and transcendence than prose paragraphs can possibly be.

COMMUNION

When breath comes quick and tongue caresses tongue,
When arms surround and hands reach out to touch
Those secret places where there is so much
Of love and longing waiting to be sprung;

When senses sing and hearts begin to race,
When rhythms quicken toward the vast surprise,
And from our depths they raise those little cries
Of joy which tell of our impending grace;

Then comes that end creation had in sight!
Yet when it comes, so delicately spun,
It sends us hurtling weightless toward the sun,
A brilliant, warming, healing place of light.

And then we lie entirely at rest,
Our hands rest lightly on each other's breast
And, by these sacramental gestures, own
Just what it is to know—and to be known.

THE CONSECRATION OF THE HOUSE

The apartment she wanted was available, so
she couldn't wait until there was furniture
enough to fill it. She moved in
with scarcely more than a table and a bed.

Did she know they would become
twin altars for a consecration?

Next night she asked him to supper,
promising improvisation:
boxes for chairs, candles in the fireplace.
April was wintry that supper eve,
and on his way to her he bought
a house-warming box of pressed logs,
replacement for their candled surrogate.

They lit a fire,
and in its coruscations
shared the tabled bread and wine,
exchanged the taste and touch
of their first communion in that house.

Then, supper done, they stretched out on the rug
before the passioning flame,
and there they drew each other into consecrate embrace,
pressed mouth to eager mouth,
felt senses fused and molten—
and took themselves in hot haste
to that other altar.

They lit a fire there, too.

Is the use of spiritual language, of the metaphor of transcendence, inappropriate in these frankly carnal verses? On the contrary, it is the most natural of languages, arising intrinsically, authentically, naturally, indeed inevitably, out of the experiences themselves; experiences which are among the most precious intimations of transcendence we can ever receive.

Love As Carnality, 2

And then what?

Nothing but blissful, satisfied subsidence, if popular portrayals in romantic novels and films are to be believed. They aren't!

What makes those portrayals objectionable isn't their sexual explicitness but their sexual fraudulence. Almost never does a hint of disappointment, to say nothing of failure, intrude in the sex they portray. Having achieved simultaneous orgasm (an achievement much over-praised in any event), the virtuoso pair are either ready for an immediate repeat engagement, or go off to sleep with smiles on their faces.

Sometimes physical intimacy does, indeed, have that result. But even under what may seem the best of circumstances, coital failure and post-coital disappointment do sometimes intrude. If we have been misled by the popular portrayals, disappointment and failure will leave us feeling personally diminished, probably angry. Rather than reproaching oneself or one's partner, we do better to try to figure out what disappointment or failure are trying to tell us about the relationship.

Here are three possibilities.

Discomfort may be a sign that we are aware, at a level deeper than conscious knowing, that the carnal act was dishonest; that it "said" more about the relationship than was really true; that once the erotic excitement was gone, there wasn't enough real residual affection left to keep things going. (There will be more about this in a later section on "Love and Marriage.") Suffice it to say here that if the intensity of post-coital affection for one's partner isn't up to the intensity of the coital arousal the two generated, that dissonance will be experienced as discomfort in the other's presence. After a night of passion, the morning finds one wishing to God she were somewhere else, or that the other was gone.

Sometimes post-coital unease, disappointment, comes because we expected too much of physical intimacy in the first place. These days we have come to anticipate that physical intimacy can deliver us from whatever most desperately besets us. The popular culture has led us to assume that if our relationships are disarrayed, the solution is to be found by rushing as quickly and as frequently as possible into sexual embrace. So into the physical act we carry all of our yearnings for satisfaction and significance in the hope of instant orgasmic transformation. It is no wonder, then, that at worst we fail, or at best that we move from climax to anti-climax. Then instead of leaving us filled, closeness only deepens the void. Physical embrace is delicate and fragile and cannot bear the whole weight of our desperation.

Moreover, there is more to intimacy than being close. "The desire to know another's nakedness," says Frederick Buechner,

> is really the desire to know the other fully as a person. It is the desire to know and to be known, not just sexually but as a total human being. It is the desire for a relationship where each gives not just of his body but of his self and spirit both, for the other's gladness.

Our embraces can confirm, deepen, and communicate intimacy; but two bodies rubbing frantically up against each other are powerless, by means of that friction alone, to create genuine intimacy *ex nihilo*. All of the technique in the world can't bridge the loneliness which grows between two people who have nothing important to say to each other.

Discomfort may arise out of the realization that, in the moment of ecstasy, more was revealed than one intended. A musical metaphor may help here. We may be good at orchestrating the tone and tempo of a relationship, keeping things in harmonious balance, permitting now this voice quality and now another to be heard. We may even attempt to orchestrate certain aspects of our physical intimacy, or find an orchestration already written out for us, planning seduction and foreplay in advance, perhaps with considerable success.

What we can't compose is the cadenza, both musically and sexually the climax of the movement. When we labor self-consciously to reach it, it eludes us. We can't create the power of the climactic moment; rather, we are carried along by that power. It is not the artist but the art that takes control, drawing out from us responses which may be surprising or shocking, ecstatic or frightened. In that sexual cadenza, emotions otherwise kept carefully in check may come pouring forth; capacities for warmth or withdrawal, for tenderness or brutality, nowhere else expressed, appear; selfishness or selflessness is unmasked; joys and fears are confirmed; needs and sufficiencies cry out which are not otherwise guessed at; language is used which, in any other context, would be inappropriate.

Even when the total effect is fulfilling, the experience may nevertheless be unsettling, precisely because it defies our conscious control and has the power to reveal, whether we wish it so or not, the dimensions of a self nowhere else exposed in quite this way.

So Paul Tillich has warned,

The ecstasy of love can absorb one's own self in its union with the other self, and separation seems to be overcome. But after these moments, the isolation of self from self is felt even more deeply than before, sometimes even to the point of mutual repulsion. We have given too much of ourselves, and now we long to take back what was given.

The experience of erotic intimacy is perhaps the most sensitive barometer we have for measuring the atmospheric pressure of a relationship. At other times and in our other experiences together, we may succeed in obscuring what our common nakedness cannot hide.

If post-coital disappointment tells us that our efforts at intimacy are dishonest, we owe it to each other to face that dishonesty frankly, either examining our relationship to see if there are in it resources for a deeper mutual commitment, or finding more appropriate—more honest—ways to be together.

If disappointment shows us that we have expected too much of orgasmic experience, we may need to understand that we are unlikely to achieve effective intercourse in the carnal sense unless there is also effective intercourse in the dialogic sense: cultivating the habit of talking with each other—hearing the words we have for each other, ready sharing with the other out of one's own depth, ready receiving from the other into one's own depth. In some circumstances, that will mean seeking professional help in identifying and eliminating the barriers to real dialogic encounter, and hence to fully-satisfying intercourse in both of its meanings.

If post-coital unease comes, on Paul Tillich's terms, out of apprehension that we may have given too much of ourselves, then we must be ready gently to reassure each other that there is safety in the relationship—safety for differences in responsiveness, safety from emotional encroachment and blaming, safety for venturing and change, safety even for failure.

Love & Virginity

$\mathcal{V}$irginity? Does anybody worry about "damaged goods"—male or female—any more? The very word "virginity" has a kind of antique sound about it, evoking a time and place that is distant and alien, given both the sexual permissiveness of recent decades and the common assumption that relationships are likely to work better if two people aren't novices at the techniques of physical intimacy.

Yet I sense a nostalgia among middle-class Americans for values, more recently repudiated, that were once standard expectations in our society, however inconsistently and imperfectly they were practiced. Virginity was one of them: the value, in a loving relationship and most especially in a prospective marriage, attached to sexual inexperience, to sexual "innocence."

Given the nostalgic trend, so-called "innocence" may come to be valued again. Just in case it is—and even if it isn't—I want to propose a redefinition of "virginity." In spite of ancient association, it is a mistake to believe that virginity is simply a matter of the genitals.

There's nothing inherently "pure" about sexual inexperience, and there's nothing inherently "impure" in sexual experience. Women and men are more than animals, and human sexuality is more than cyclical heat. It can be, rather, an occasion for the most exquisite tenderness, for intense pleasure intensely shared, for the deepest communion between two people, for the confirmation of our identity as man, as woman, for a willing act of co-creation.

Surely it is fulfillment, not defilement, which can be found in such "knowing" of another human being.

Virginity is a moral matter, not a physiological one. Its proper meaning is not inexperience but wholeness, purity only in the sense of integrity. Loss of virginity does not necessarily occur in some primal sexual encounter. We can't know whether or not the bare fact of intercourse, whether the first time or the tenth, is morally significant until we examine the quality of the relationship within which it occurs.

Virginity is lost, is absent, only when integrity is broken because a sexual relationship is dishonest.

Given this definition, there is no escape from asserting that there are both sexually experienced virgins and sexually inexperienced men and women who have given up their virginity. For the former, the sexual relationship has integrity because it is an honest expression of the true spiritual relationship that exists between two people. For the latter, in spite of an actual relationship which has the appearance of full and continuing mutual responsibility, one partner or both refuse to become "one flesh," to participate in the sexual act which is the most appropriate and powerful symbol—the consummation—of that mutuality.

To "say" too little about a relationship is as much a lie as it is to "say" too much.

Virginity is the presence of relational wholeness, of relational integrity. It is lost only when wholeness has been broken by acts of sexual dishonesty, within the relationship or outside of it. But virginity can be recovered, and love regained, in the giving and accepting of the gift of forgiveness, whose power it is to heal what has been broken, and to make lives whole again.

Love & Forgiveness

There is in love a kind of nakedness for which we may not have bargained.

The physical nakedness which goes with the sexual kind of "making love" may appeal to us or not, depending on a complex of personal psychological factors. But to "make love" in the larger sense requires a moral nakedness which even the most eager lover may find difficult to accept.

Relationships are fragile. Even in the very best of circumstances, things go wrong, sometimes thoughtlessly and inadvertently, at other times impulsively and deliberately. Love can only grow, can only be sustained in us and among us, where there is both the will to forgive, and the willingness to be forgiven.

It's important to be clear that forgiveness does not mean to overlook or to forget. To do either is to pretend that violations of relational intimacy aren't real, aren't serious. They are! No loving relationship is possible for us where our offenses against intimacy go unacknowledged, as if they didn't matter. They do! And no loving restoration is possible without the memory of offense, which reduces the likelihood that it will happen again.

Pretense and lies—the lie that it didn't happen, or the pretense that it doesn't matter—whether told to oneself or to the other, feed exploitation. Love is bound to truth.

Stripped of its sentimental accretions, forgiveness is essentially truth-telling and truth-hearing. It means, if I have been hurt by some action or inaction of my beloved, that I must be willing to say, as soon as possible, and as directly and specifically as I can, what that hurt is. Depending on the nature of the hurt, that truth-telling may be accompanied by some anger. And I must make it clear, despite my hurt and anger, that I am prepared to keep all of the human options open between us. That's what forgiveness is.

If, on the other hand, I have caused the hurt in my beloved by my action or inaction, I must be prepared to hear her hurt, including her anger, and to respond with my own truth-telling by acknowledging my offense, the appropriateness of her anger, and my determination that the hurt shall not be repeated. Doing that means I am willing to receive her forgiveness.

If I'm the one who has been hurt, I must be prepared to do my own hearing: I must hear the acknowledgement and the pledge, and having heard them, I must be prepared to let my hurt go. Doing that is not only to offer forgiveness; it is to act forgivingly.

No relationship can survive in which hurts are held and nurtured by the offended one, where there is something in the relationship that has to be lived down. Similarly, no relationship can survive in which the offender refuses to hear and acknowledge the truth of his offenses. Love can grow only where forgiveness is both given and received, which means that, rather than having something to live down, the offender has found someone to live with.

Forgiveness is both tough to give and tough to accept because it entails a certain moral nakedness. For the offender, it means finding the grace to acknowledge that he has violated the privileged intimacy to which he has been admitted in the relationship. And that kind of admission of fault—that kind of baring of the soul—doesn't come easily.

Offering forgiveness is also tough to do. It's hard to give up the satisfaction that comes from a feeling of moral superiority in the presence of the offender; even hard to give up the momentary satisfaction of wounded pride. But such feeling is like the snake that swallows its own tail: there is some nourishment in it, but it is definitely subject to the law of diminishing returns.

And offering forgiveness carries its own kind of vulnerability, its own kind of moral nakedness. No one is likely to be equal to it who cannot say what I recently heard a workshop participant say in discussing this problem. Commenting on the behavior of another person, a behavior she found particularly offensive, she said, "I must learn to accept the person in me who does the very same thing."

Stripped to our human essentials, offender and offended one are very much alike. And while responsibility for an offense against intimacy, though uneven, is seldom entirely onesided, it is this recognition that makes the offering of forgiveness possible. Blaise Pascal expressed the daring act of the imagination on which such forgiveness depends, when he said that I must always consider the offender,

> so long as he is alive, capable of being illuminated by grace, and to believe that in a short while he may be fuller of faith than I myself, while I, on the other hand, may fall into the blindness which is now his.

Having said all of that, one more thing must be said. For some, the cost of forgiveness—its moral nakedness—is too great. Sometimes, though it would be gladly received, it is withheld; sometimes, having been gladly offered, it is refused. And then there may be nothing to do except to acknowledge that the relationship is irretrievably broken. Forgiveness can work miracles, but it is not a kind of magic that works in spite of us.

On the one hand, as the offender I am powerless by myself to restore to wholeness a relationship which, by my own arbitrary action, I have broken. A relationship that has been violated can never be retrieved. It can only be received. It cannot be taken back by me. It must be given back to me.

On the other hand, as the offended one, I cannot give a gift for which there is no willing recipient.

Life is always a gift, whether in that act in which we are first created, or in those continuing acts of forgiveness by means of which our lives must continually be restored and renewed. Forgiveness is the cement which holds life together, since it is the refusal to accept any relationship as permanently broken.

In spite of the risk, the vulnerability, the moral nakedness forgiveness requires, our lives are in ultimate danger only if we refuse to offer each other the gift of life, only if we refuse to receive that gift from each other.

And when forgiveness is both offered and received, it can, indeed, work miracles.

Love & Friendship

We were talking about mutual friends, a woman and a man who had recently married. I said it would never have occurred to me in advance that she would see him as a desirable marriage partner.

My companion agreed that, on the face of it, he was an unlikely match for her aspiration, and then added, "For a long time she held out for a relationship that had dash and romance. But every time she found one, it didn't last. Finally she came to the conclusion, that there's a lot to be said for marrying your best friend."

Recently I helped two friends celebrate their twenty-fifth wedding anniversary. I didn't know them twenty-five years ago, and I don't know whether or not there was dash and romance in their early relationship. What I do know is that that relationship has lasted these twenty-five years because there is, at its heart, deep friendship.

That has to be true for any relationship to last—especially for a marriage really to be a marriage, a literal "wedding," and not merely a condition of simultaneity without intimacy. Friendship: marked by shared commitments, shared passions; and marked by respected differences, too—differences of talent, of temperament, such that, over time, each marriage partner can grow out of what the other has to give.

Remember what St. Exupéry said about love—that it's not two people looking passionately at each other, but rather two people looking passionately together at the world? That's what friendship is at its depth. That's what lasts!

Friendship is what sustains us when romance is regularly crowded out by routine. Friendship is what makes forgiveness possible when tensions temporarily unbalance. Friendship had better be there when the children are grown and gone. Friendship is the reality that remains for us when dreams are disappointed.

The most successful marriages give testimony to the wise observation, that there's a lot to be said for marrying your best friend.

Marriage apart, there is one other important thing that ought to be said about friendship. It has to do with individuals who have deliberately chosen celibacy or who, for whatever reason, may be temporarily or permanently without a committed, conjugal relationship. Are they destined, then, to stand outside of the circle of love, never to be "lover" or to know the delight that comes in offering and receiving the tenderest of spoken gifts, "I love you"?

Not necessarily so at all. I know a man and a woman who have no hesitation in saying "I love you" to each other at those moments when they experience the depth of their caring for each other. As it happens, she is married, he is not, but they could be any two people anywhere. Theirs is not, and will never become, a romantic relationship. Not even in private fantasy does either of them imagine that it could be otherwise. Each knows what "I love you" means and what it doesn't mean.

What they have is a friendship of remarkable depth that joins *eros, philia,* and *agape*—one in which he honors and respects her commitment to her husband (who is also his friend), and in which she honors and respects his active reaching out to other women who may be potential marriage partners.

What is missing for the celibate, or for the one who is without a conjugal relationship temporarily or otherwise, is *epithymia*, explicitly sexual love. And while those of us who have been graced by its ecstasy may think it sad that anyone should fail to experience such transcendent knowing, such exquisite pleasure, it is no small thing in a friendship when *eros, philia,* and *agape* come together, making it possible for two people to speak to each other, with honesty and integrity, those incredibly confirming and humanizing words: "I love you."

FOUR

Love's Gifts

Playfulness

A French translator has rendered one of the New Testament Beatitudes as "Blessed are the debonair" [Matthew 5:5a]. To a reader who is accustomed to the Authorized Version's "Blessed are the meek," the alteration startles. Yet surely the instinct of the translator was as sound as it was daring.

Clearly the passage intends to say that genuine love of God leads to a life of care-less abandon and to a kind of spontaneous gaiety. It is not the "timid" but the "debonair" who are blessed: those who have been lifted above the cares of this world by a world-changing, joy-infusing love.

There is, as well in my love for another human being, something that is extraordinarily freeing, world-altering, joy-infusing. At important moments, in the presence of the loved one I am pervaded by an optimism, a confidence in the life-process, that permits me to experience care-less abandon, as if all were "right with the world." Because at important moments the lover and I are the world. If we can't—indeed, if we shouldn't—take so exclusive and excluding a view except momentarily, that doesn't minimize the importance of those blithe hours when ordinary concerns disappear and the lover and I are able to be together, to play together, with the singleminded innocence of childhood, as if we hadn't a care in the world.

METAMORPHOSIS OVER SHAWNEE MISSION PARK

It was an unlikely candidate for flight,
your kite.
Eight inches (scarcely more) of styrofoam
no thicker than a comb—
that frail!—
with several yards of tail
to give it an ungainly
aspect. Vainly,
it seemed, could that craft hope to soar
above the meadow floor.

"It will never fly, Wilbur," I said.
(When we're in bed,
rising on some thermal draft of passion,
it is my fashion
to call you by a tenderer female name.)
All the same,
it flew, that kite, reducing my smug male prediction
to instant fiction!
Once cast aloft, it skittered like a thing
possessed, drawn ever higher on an eerie, aerie wing.
Its tail of Chinese red
moved in a dizzying, dervish delirium, fed
by spirited currents of air
invisible to that quite unspiritual pair
who stood below.
(That's you and me, in case you didn't know.)

Later we drew it, resisting, down to settle
in flowering nettle.
And what, that magic hour of flight, had been
         an enchanting spastic,
was disenchanted string and plastic.

Vividness

It is the common testimony of poetry and song, that love sharpens our senses and sensibilities. Days seem brighter, nights fuller of mystery, memories more luminous, dreams more real, and the ordinary—even what is ordinary in the lover—quite extraordinary.

SLEEPLESS IN SEATTLE

All the way home last night
I breathed your presence
where cheek had touched lucky cheek
with the sweet scent of remembrance.

Now in the early darkness of my waking,
just five short hours since we rose
from our first real embrace,
I taste again the gentle passioning
of your mouth,
feel the delicious ache of you
in my breast, and hear
in your whispered name an exultant new
bene-diction.

URSA MAJOR

Did we really happen, you and I?
Or were those luminous hours a chimera
spun out of my mere yearning?

Are you real, or was it my mind that teased
with gentle, tender mocking?

Was it you I touched as we walked the wooded path?
Could I have imagined the bear that permitted us—
less self-conscious, in feigned fright—
to put hand into ready hand?

Did we really talk of serious things,
or was my sense of substance,
of the mind's intimate companionship,
something only wished for?

It all seemed intensely real, intensely good—
so good, I wonder now if I have only dreamed it:
> *the beguiling tease,*
> *the warming touch,*
> *the illuminating talk.*

Perhaps there's only one way to be sure.
Please meet me again.
There will be bears!

ANOMALIES: FINDING YOU HERE ON WAKING ALONE

We slept together last night,
you and I.

Virginly, though the penetration
was deep.

No reversal of roles, yet you
inside of me.

Not merely merging flesh with secret
flesh, but in my breathing, pulsing,
metabolizing, dreaming.

Consummation without climax,
our intercourse barely weeks old.

No innocence lost;
wonder regained.

Unconditional Surrender

$\mathcal{I}$t is rare, and quite wonderful, to experience in our ordinarily regulated and routinized lives a capacity for radical openness—a complete taking in, a complete giving away. Such an experience comes at times of crisis, when some kind of heroism is the only adequate response. It comes more often in the experience of love, at moments when we are so overwhelmed by the sheer unimaginableness, the miracle, of loving and being loved, that nothing less than total surrender to the lover, from the lover, seems possible.

ALL'S FAIR

When some silent
Lissome loveliness leaps
Upon my senses I cry:
No quarter given
And none taken!

Restraint

If love opens us up to uncalculated acts of daring, both of commitment and of surrender, it can also bring out a capacity for great delicacy—not because the relationship is fragile, but because it is precious and awakens in us a respect to match our passion.

GOING ALL THE WAY

"How do you tell someone
that even something as nice as this
should stop," she told him.

It was a tender stroke,
as tender in its way as the touch
with which he had caressed her.

Gentle strength,
her words set limits without rebuke.
She kept her proportion
and let him keep her thanks
for warmth without heat.

Rare intercourse!

Pain

Divorce I

It's daybreak now in Winter Park.
She's stirring out of heavy sleep
And stretching lovely legs and arms
That nights and nights have held me deep.

It's noontime there, and in the sun
She lies in wait for supple tan
And presses wantonly to earth
The breasts that once caressed my hand.

It's evening now in Winter Park.
She studies propped upon her bed
And concentrates her will and wit
On which my wit and will have fed.

It's midnight there, and sleep has spilled
Her out across the counterpane.
And sleep might overtake me, too,
If only we could love again.

For real as seem these vivid scenes
Of how my once-love spends her day,
They're dreams. She lives in Winter Park,
And I a thousand miles away.

DIVORCE II

"The pain is here, near my heart,"
he said.
"Have you had it before?
the doctor asked.
"Yes," he replied.
"Well," she diagnosed,
"you've got it again."

Pain, one of the *gifts* of love? Is that a misprint?

Hard as it may be to accept at first, the pain which sometimes arises out of genuine love—even out of lost love—is indeed a gift. To insulate oneself against love because it runs the risk of pain is to miss one of the richest experiences life can offer.

To be sure, there is a great deal of nonsense spoken, in conventional religious circles, about the relation of suffering to the spiritual life. The notion, for example, that one ought to seek suffering because it's a sign of some supposed spiritual nobility, is perverse. There's no nobility in self-victimization. Willingness to "take up a cross" doesn't mean going out in search of crucifixion. It means, rather, a refusal to be deterred from right action merely because that action may have emotional cost, may even entail risk to life and limb.

The contrary prevailing secular notion—that all suffering is to be avoided, instantly anesthetized, tranquilized—is equally perverse. There is yet another way to understand suffering—a way more humanly promising—that relates to our reconsideration of love. There are some forms of suffering that are gifts, not to be sentimentalized or wallowed in, but to be received with gratitude.

In 1986, when my wife's mother died unexpectedly in her sleep, my wife's grief was immediate, agonizing, painful. How could it have been otherwise, given the love she had felt for her mother? Her grief was a testimony to what she had been given in that relationship over a span of 42 years. Her willingness to experience that suffering fully was, and continues to be, her mother's most touching and telling memorial. And it made on me an absolutely indelible impression.

Such an understanding of suffering doesn't come easily, as I have personal reason to know. Yet when it comes, it brings a certain liberation. At this writing, I am six years into an unwelcome divorce, after a relationship that reached back nearly 25 years. Largely, I think, because of my wife's example at the time of her mother's death, I have come to experience my own pain and loss differently from the way I would have experienced it prior to 1986. I now understand that the suffering I have experienced in the presence of my own loss is the consequence of the gift my wife gave me throughout those 25 years, and that my proper response to that pain is not only regret at her loss but gratitude for her gift.

It is clear to me that the secret of competent suffering—whatever its source—lies in the meaning that suffering discloses. Suffering that results from abusiveness and brutality is devoid of meaning—is destructive of meaning—and ought not be endured if meaning is ever to be recovered for the abused or the abuser. Suffering that results from the ravages of disease can be endured only if values are present that are deeper than mere ease. Suffering that comes from brave action can be borne only if the cause is large enough.

The pain that results from the loss of love can be received with gratitude when we understand it as the most touching and telling evidence of the genuineness of that love; only when we accept it as the mark of a gift we were given in that love—a gift so precious that we can never wish the experience to have been otherwise.

NEVER YOU

Kiri Te Kanawa and André Previn were
a menace to drivers on Interstate 5
this afternoon.

Or rather, I was the menace,
driving with tears dimming my visual field
as that evocative pair told me how
"Love is lovelier the second time around."
It was.
"It could happen to you," *Kiri warned.*
It did.
"It's easy to remember, but so hard to forget,"
she sang—as if I didn't know.

Her voice reached an old
yet ever-fresh wound in my depth:
"I've been running through rain
and the wind that follows after,
for one certain face,
and an unforgotten laughter...

"Yes, I looked everywhere
you can look without wings,
and I found a great variety
of interesting things.

"But it never was you.
It never was anywhere you."

That's when the tears came.

Will it always be this way? Probably.
You touched, awakened something in me
that I had never felt before. It was what
I had always thought joy might feel like,
if ever I came upon it, if ever it came upon me.
I keep hoping it will find me again, and I
look for it in every face I see.

But it never is you.
It never is anywhere you.

Then would I forget you if I could, drive out
the pain of remembering, stanch the reckless
tears Kiri and André drew from me as I drove
this afternoon? But they were, after all, tears
drawn out of joy.

Were it not for you,
there would be nothing worth crying about.

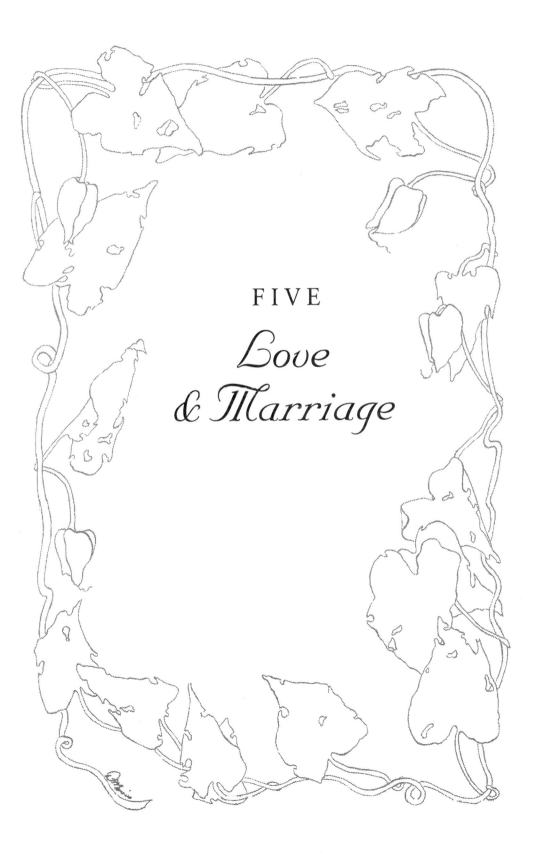

FIVE

Love & Marriage

A Wedding Invocation

Come, coursing planets and coruscating stars,
and cast your mystery upon this magic moment.

Come, quaternary winds and surging tides,
and link our human pulses to the primordial
rhythms of the universe.

Come, friendly spirits of the animal world,
and celebrate with us the goodness that is in all living.

Come, dear friends of these two, and witness
to the promises they will make to each other,
and the new estate into which they purpose
now to enter.

Come, mothering and fathering Spirit of the universe.
By your love, create for us here a sacred space,
and bless with loving consequence
what we are about to do in it.

The Marriage Ceremony: Antiquarian Throwback?

The marriage ceremony is a strange ritual indeed, to judge by contemporary standards of behavior.

Says one observer, "Who would argue that the vows exchanged at weddings are anything but wild and improbable ...unrealistic at best, hypocritical at worst."

Just think of it: promising an intimacy that will be exclusive—monogamous—in a time when simultaneous intimacies no longer scandalize; promising a bond that will be lifelong, in a time when most things—relationships as well as computers and refrigerators—are only expected to last a relatively short time, and when marriage partners are traded in as easily and unregrettably as automobiles.

Come to that, the idea that in order to live together a couple should have a public, ceremonial authorization will seem to some to be an anachronism, in a time when unsanctioned cohabitation is probably as common as the sanctioned kind.

At the risk of appearing quaint and antiquarian, I want to suggest that it may be the easy intimacies and traded partnerships that are unrealistic, and that the public, ceremonial commitment of one life to another, far from being anachronistic and old-fashioned, is one of the things that makes sustained and successful living together possible.

Help for Keeping Promises

$\mathcal{W}$hat can be said in favor of ceremonializing marriage? Clearly, there are many who are less than certain that the liturgical foofaraw of a wedding service is really necessary.

This can be said: No marriage is ever a purely private affair, regardless of the circumstances in which it may occur. Because marriage involves two people in their totality, because it leaves no aspect of their being untouched, it reaches into as many lives and alters as many relationships as the two represent in their totality.

A wedding ceremony is nothing more than a proper acknowledgement that marriage is simply not a private affair, that it matters to more than the two who come to be joined. In an important sense others have a stake in it too. When the marriage pair exchange their vows in the presence of those others—families, friends—the two not only make their promises to each other but as well to the community they have gathered there. They enter into an implicit covenant with those witnesses for the faithful fulfillment of what they have promised to each other.

Traditional ceremonies, seldom used these days, gave specific acknowledgement to the active role of the community in marriage. The officiant asked, "If there be anyone here who knows any just cause why these two should not be lawfully joined in marriage, let him speak now or forever after hold his peace." These days that question is usually not asked, because officiants accept it as their responsibility to identify any impediments to the marriage in advance of the ceremony itself. But the implicit public covenant remains; otherwise why have anyone else there? After all, a marriage service is not a performance to which one invites an audience. It is, rather, a ritual event, at once solemn and celebratory, in which promises are made, witnessed, and, in that witnessing, confirmed.

If anyone should wonder what real difference all that makes, the author of the Epistle to the Hebrews in the New Testament has an answer: "Therefore, since we are surrounded by so great a cloud of witnesses, let us also lay aside every weight and the sin that clings so closely, and let us run with perseverance the race that is set before us." [12:1]

Given the pressure of the times in favor of instant gratification, given the popular view that there is no vow so serious that we may not break it if it becomes inconvenient, and given the inclination we all have to regard our narrow self-interest above any other interests, we need all the help we can get to keep our promises.

And that's another reason the rest of us are there. Gabriel Marcel said that when something is expected of us, we are given hope, because the very fact of the confidence expressed in us by the expectation confers on us the power to fulfill what is expected. The presence of a gathered community surrounds the marriage pair with loving and empowering expectations.

Seeing that they are surrounded by so great a cloud of witnesses, what they promise really can come true.

Staying Power For Tough Times

What can be said in favor of the vow, that the wedding promises two people make to each other shall hold "as long as they both shall live"?

This can be said: All living together is difficult. It is not a natural talent; it is something we have to learn to do. Furthermore, however much a marriage may bring moments of delight, it will also bring moments of discouragement; ecstasy there will be, and agony as well.

This has always been so; but there is something peculiarly contemporary that demands our consideration here. Our times give us a good conscience about expecting, insisting on, instant gratification, and about rejecting whatever fails to gratify us instantly. So there is danger that, at moments when living together is difficult, when it is discouraging, even agonizing, our first impulse may be to give it up, the way we would trade in a cranky car, move from a house that doesn't give us enough room, change a hair style we've grown tired of.

How many people do you know who move through their lives from one temporary relationship to another in a futile search for a gratification that doesn't have to be worked at? Well, in human relationships there is no such thing as gratification that doesn't have to be worked at.

So when, in the marriage service, two people make their promises "as long as we both shall live," that is a way of saying,

"Somewhere I will find the strength to see you through your rough times, and I ask you for the strength to see me through mine."

It is an acknowledgement that, far from being burdens to be escaped from, rough times are really gifts, moments of privilege that offer real intimacy, real bonding; that give us access to each other with a richness which not even sexual ecstasy can match; that allow us to know each other at levels deeper even than sexual knowing; that allow us even to know ourselves and our capacity for giving at a level deeper than we could otherwise have imagined.

Keeping Intimacy Honest

*W*hat can be said in favor of the vow of faithfulness two people make to each other in the wedding service?

This can be said: The way we behave in each other's presence is either appropriate or inappropriate depending on whether or not that behavior honestly symbolizes the nature of the relationship within which it occurs. If I am warmly embraced by a total stranger whom I meet under the most casual of circumstances, that embrace is a dishonest symbol of our actual relationship. If I casually shake my wife's hand on first being reunited with her after a long and regretted absence, that too is symbolically dishonest.

Whatever else it may be, sexual intimacy is inescapably a form of symbolic communication. It is appropriate only when what it "says" about a relationship is really true; it is inappropriate whenever it "says" more about a relationship than can honestly be said. Because sexual intimacy is so critical to our humanity—because it has such power to confirm or disconfirm our identities as men and women, because it releases emotions and impulses which otherwise we manage to hold in check, because in it we are more vulnerable, physically and spiritually, than at almost any other moment of our lives—it can be safely entered into only in a relationship which is so structured as to bear that intensity, that vulnerability, that intimate disclosure, and their continuing effects upon the two people involved long after the orgasmic shudders have ceased.

So, in the words of a theologian whom I admire, since sexual intimacy "involves such utter self-giving, such utter commitment and concern for the other, it can honestly express only a relationship which itself knows humility, trust, and selflessness."

Sexual intimacy is therefore an honest symbol only in a relationship in which two people are both willing and able to sustain and endure, to take delight in and growth from, the most continuous, varied, intimate, and all-embracing being together. That's what marriage is about. In any context less serious and less whole, sexual intimacy is simply dishonest.

Who Marries Whom, When?

In spite of all that can be said in support of what a marriage service publicly declares, there is something presumptuous in it as well.

The presumption is in the conventionally accepted notion that the two who present themselves are to be married by the officiant, whoever that person may be—minister, priest, rabbi, judge or justice of the peace, even ocean-liner captain.

The truth is that no cleric, no civil official, can marry the two who come before him. Only those two can marry themselves. Only they can covenant together "for better, for worse."

The most an officiant can do—and the rest of us are there to join in as well—is to bless, affirm and confirm, and celebrate the marrying which the bride and groom have already begun; the marrying that will be their loving daily work throughout their life together.

A wedding ceremony is a reminder of our need for each other; the need for each other of the two who are there to be joined, to be sure; and the need the rest of us have for the other, as well. A marriage ceremony is a celebration of selfhood as a lifelong gift we give to each other.

There are, in our time, those who believe that the basic human unit is one person. But marriage is a celebration for those, rather, who understand that the self and the other—you and I—are not separable realities but a single miracle.

Doing The Undoable

After everything has been said about marriage, one thing remains to be said. It was touched on at the end of the very first chapter on "Locating Love," and now it brings our reflections full circle.

Here it is: Measured by ordinary standards, marriage is simply an undoable estate. On the face of it, the likelihood of success in marriage wouldn't seem to be very high.

Just consider. After years in which two people have attended almost exclusively to their own individual needs and responded to their own individual inclinations, after having looked daily into the mirror and found only a single image reflected there, now by instant decree of church and state each finds it necessary to make room for another reflection in a mirror that has grown no larger after the wedding ceremony than it was before.

After years in which two people have hidden their individual private lives from the view of the world, and have told themselves that if ever anybody else knew what they were really like the sky would fall, suddenly by instant decree of church and state somebody else is close enough to know.

So the ability to enter successfully into the wedded estate is not a natural talent. As we have already seen, willingness to displace oneself in order to share life's center with another does not come easily. Vulnerability to the intimate knowledge of another is risky, scary.

Then how does marriage ever work? Sometimes, of course, it doesn't, when selfishness has grown too deep or self-disgust too strong. But marriage can work, does work—works, I suspect, more often than not. And when it does, the secret ingredient is grace.

Grace is a religious term. The theologian Paul Tillich once said, "There is a grace in life. Otherwise we could not live." And one of the things he meant was that the creative process in the universe—what some call God—intends and supports our good; that in the end love lasts, as Paul said in I Corinthians 13; that although individual relationships may come to an end, love's influence is nevertheless indelible.

And grace is also a profoundly human term, though that connection isn't often enough made. In more ways than we can ever imagine, and in more ways than we can ever acknowledge, life itself is a gift given to us both by those we know and by others we will never know. And when we live well, the credit is only partly our own; it is in larger part unearned income from the generosity of others.

When marriage succeeds, it is a work of grace. It is the result of the capacity each of us has, not only to give to another, but to receive from another, which is often even harder; the capacity not only to accept but to be accepted, which is often even harder. When marriage succeeds, it is the product of generosity and humility: the generosity that gives without strings, the humility that receives without strings.

John le Carré has written that "...there is no reward for love except the experience of loving, and nothing to be learned by it except humility." Beyond mere romanticism, that's really what love is all about.

Afterword

Friend, let this be enough. If thou wouldst go on reading,
Go and thyself become the writing and the meaning.
                                                —Angelus Silesius

Notes On Writers & Books

*A*lthough my text does not contain footnotes, I am eager for readers to have access to the writers who have inspired me with their wisdom about life and loving. Consulting them, however, should not be a substitute for one's own getting on with "becoming the writing and the meaning," as Angelus Silesius urges in the Afterword.

KINGSLEY AMIS (1922-) is a prolific English novelist, best known for his brilliant academic satire, *Lucky Jim* (1953). *The Russian Girl*, from which the quotation in "Love: 'In,' or on Its Way 'Out'?" is taken, was written in 1992, and *I Want It Now*, cited in "Love Is Hard Work," was written in 1968.

ANGELUS SILESIUS, a.k.a. Johannes Scheffler (1624-1677) was a religious poet, hymn writer, and mystic. Originally a Lutheran, he converted to Roman Catholicism. The quotation in the Afterword is from *Cherubic Wayfarer* (1674).

DIETRICH BONHOEFFER (1906-1945), a German Protestant theologian, was imprisoned for alleged involvement in the plot to overthrow Hitler, and was executed just days before his prison camp was liberated by American forces. His most popular work, published posthumously, is *Letters and Papers from Prison* (1953), from which the quotation in "Love as Carnality, I" is taken.

MARTIN BUBER (1878-1965) was a Jewish philosopher who fled from Germany to Jerusalem in 1938, and taught subsequently at Hebrew University. His classic *I and Thou* (1923)—the lines quoted in "We Need Each Other" and "Love and Selfhood" are from that work—has had a profound influence on both Jewish and Christian spirituality and theology.

FREDERICK BUECHNER (1926-) is a widely-read novelist, theologian, and autobiographer, whose books have been Pulitzer and National Book Award nominees. The quotation in "Our Need for Each Other" is from *A Room Called Remember* (1984), the one in "Love and Carnality, II" is from *The Hungering Dark* (1969).

JOHN LE CARRÉ (1931-) is the celebrated author of such novels of intrigue as *The Spy Who Came In from the Cold* (1963), and more recently *A Perfect Spy* (1986), *The Russia House* (1989), and *The Night Manager* (1993), which contain some of the tenderest and most touching passages about love to be found in contemporary fiction. The quotation in "Doing the Undoable" is from *The Secret Pilgrim* (1991).

KAHLIL GIBRAN (1883-1931) was a Lebanese mystic whose blend of Eastern and Western spirituality took its most popular form in *The Prophet* (1923), which has nurtured several generations in their spiritual quests.

Habits of the Heart (1985) was a report on research into the American character conducted by five scholars led by sociologist ROBERT BELLAH. It is one of the most incisive and important interpretations since Alexis de Toqueville's *Democracy in America*, written 150 years earlier.

HENDRIK IBSEN (1828-1906) was a Norwegian dramatist whose works include *A Doll's House* (1879) and *Hedda Gabler* (1884), in addition to *Peer Gynt* (1867) and others. A major figure in the modern theater, Ibsen was also a man ahead of his time in his social views, anticipating the later work of Martin Buber and other interpersonal philosophers, and giving dramatic expression to views that would later be called feminist.

GARRISON KEILLOR (1942-) is a master storyteller, who has made Lake Wobegon, his mythical hometown in Minnesota, palpably real for millions of listeners to his "Prairie Home Companion" on National Public Radio. Stories from the program have been published in *Lake Wobegon Days* (1985) and *Leaving Home* (1987), among other books and tapes. The quotation in "Love and Selfhood" is from "Pastor Ingqvist's Trip to Orlando," in *Gospel Birds and Other Stories of Lake Wobegon* (1985).

GABRIEL MARCEL (1889-1973) was a French Catholic existentialist philosopher of wide influence. Among a great many other works, he wrote *The Philosophy of Existence* (1948), *The Mystery of Being* (1951), *Men Against Humanity* (1952), and *The Philosophy of Existentialism* (1961). I have been unable to locate the source of the quotation in "Love Expects."

JAMES F. MASTERSON (1926-), director of the Masterson Group and an attending psychiatrist at the Payne-Whitney Clinic, New York Hospital, is internationally known a psychiatric clinician, author, and researcher. The quotation in the section on "Self-Love, Other-Love" is from his chapter on "The Challenge of Intimacy" in *The Search for the Real Self: Unmasking the Personality Disorders of Our Age* (1988).

H. RICHARD NIEBUHR (1894-1962) taught theology and ethics at Yale and was one of the century's most influential moral philosophers. The quotation in the chapter on "Love and Selfhood" is from *The Responsible Self* (1963).

BLAISE PASCAL (1623-1662), a French scientist (he experimented early with measurements of barometric pressure) and mathematician (he founded the modern theory of probability and influenced the advance of differential calculus), was also a religious philosopher known especially for *The Pensées* (1670), his posthumously collected aphorisms and reflections.

ANTOINE DE SAINT EXUPÉRY (1900-1944) is best known for his popular fable, *The Little Prince* (1943). A French aviator, he was lost in action late in World War II. I have been unable to locate the source from which the quotation in the poem, "Seeing in Love," is taken.

DAME KIRI TE KANAWA, world-famed Maori operatic soprano, was introduced to singing contemporary ballads by André Previn who, in addition to having conducted symphony orchestras in London, Pittsburgh, and elsewhere, is a distinguished jazz pianist. In describing how "Pain" may be among "Love's Gifts," the lyrics quoted in the poem "Never You" are from the ballad, "It Never Was You," music and words by Kurt Weill and Maxwell Anderson, recorded on *Kiri Sidetracks: The Jazz Album* (Philips) by Kiri Te Kanawa and André Previn, with Mundell Lowe and Ray Brown.

PAUL TILLICH (1886-1965), a German academic theologian, was dismissed from his university post by the Nazis and came to this country to teach in 1933. One of the century's most influential thinkers, his impact reached far beyond conventional theological circles into such fields as art criticism, psychotherapy, and secular philosophy. His work is most accessible through his three volumes of sermons. The quotations in "Love's Other Abuse" and in "Love and Carnality, II" are from *The Eternal Now* (1963); the quotation in "Doing the Undoable" is from *The Shaking of the Foundations* (1948).